A Daughter's Broken Heart
and the Daddy Who Restored It

Amanda Tungseth

ISBN 978-1-0980-4709-2 (paperback)
ISBN 978-1-0980-4710-8 (hardcover)
ISBN 978-1-0980-4711-5 (digital)

Christian Faith Publishing, Inc.
832 Park Avenue
Meadville, PA 16335
www.christianfaithpublishing.com

Cover art by: Christine Foster

Printed in the United States of America

This book is for all the women who have been wounded because of the brokenness of their earthly daddies. You have a Heavenly Daddy who loves you more than you can imagine and would love to heal all of your hurt and pain if you will let Him.

Preface

When God first put the idea for this book on my heart, it was during one of the biggest storms of bitterness and anger I have gone through with my earthly father. I thought, *When I am completely healed from all the hurts, I will write this book.* As I thought about it more and prayed about it more, the answer was *now*. My relationship with my dad may never be fully restored the way that I would like it to be on earth, and yours may never be either. A true relationship with Christ is the only way that we can feel complete, even when our earthly relationships are broken.

This book was not written to condemn my dad. I pray for him continuously. I know that he is a broken person just like me, and that is the reason why he has made many of the choices he has in his life. I love him and hope that one day he can be set free from his brokenness and addictions. We are all broken and in need of Christ, each and every one of us.

Daddy's Little Princess

I love watching my eight-year-old daughter, Tyla, with her daddy. My husband, Josh, is what I would call the best daddy in the world. It is so precious to watch how much he adores our daughter and loves her unconditionally. He tells her she is beautiful and special. He snuggles with her. He sits and listens to her as she explains in great detail about pictures she draws and Lego creations she comes up with. He takes her on daddy-daughter dates. He answers her many, many questions lovingly, without making her feel like her questions are dumb or a waste of his time. He provides for her and makes sure her earthly needs are met. He talks to her about how important a relationship with Jesus is. She is her Daddy's Little Princess.

I know that Tyla will never have to question her daddy's love for her. The awesome thing is he isn't even her biological father. He adopted her when she was two, a few months after we got married. You would never know it though. He loves her so much, and it often brings tears to his eyes when he is talking about how she is growing so quickly or about something she did that made him proud. I believe he loves her the way God intended fathers to love their daughters.

For many of you, this may sound familiar. Maybe you had a wonderful daddy growing up, or maybe your husband is a wonderful daddy to your daughter. On the other hand, for many of you, this may make you angry. Maybe when you were a child, you were like me and longed to be Daddy's Little Princess. Maybe the hurts are so deep that you have spent your whole life searching to be loved, to find someone to fill the void your father left in your life, and to be loved the way you always dreamed of. That was me. If you picked up this book, I am guessing that *was* or *is* you too. My prayer in writing this book is that it will help you on your journey in healing, healing from the wounds left by your earthly daddy—the wounds you thought could never be patched. My greatest prayer in writing this is that you would be able to grasp the infinite love of our Heavenly Father. For some of you, this may be the point where you want to close this book and never pick it up again. If you have a negative view on God or feel like He has disappointed you in the past, please don't stop reading. I have been there and had those same feelings too. Keep on reading because this book was written for *you*!

The Early Years

Growing up, I was a very shy child. I was always feeling self-conscious and worried about what people were thinking of me—terrified of ever being asked a question in a group or having to be put in situations where I would have to be away from my mom and meet new people.

I was raised in a home with two parents and my brother who is three years younger than me. My mom worked as a hairstylist, and my dad had a roofing business. We didn't have a lot of extra money, and I remember always being concerned as a child that we didn't have enough money, but we got by.

On the outside, we looked like a happy family. We strolled into church every Sunday with our happy faces on even if my dad had been out drinking the night before and we were crying on the inside because we knew how much it hurt our mom. I learned from watching my mom at a young age to put on my happy face and pretend that nothing was wrong, even if you were hurting on the inside. It's just what we did to try to hide the hurt and dysfunction our family experienced from my dad's alcoholism.

I was a very observant child. My aunt tells me I've always been nosy. I think it started as a very young child, trying to protect my mom. I knew when something was wrong and wanted to find out why she was sad. I was always worried about her. Although she would pretend that everything was fine, I knew when something was hurting her. Most of the time it was because of my dad's drinking and the way he treated her.

My dad wasn't what most people think of when they think of an alcoholic—someone who gets drunk each and every day. I remember him always having at least a couple of beers every day after work, but he didn't get drunk every day. Most of the time, it was on a weekend with friends or even by himself in the garage. Sometimes I think not knowing when his next binge would be was worse than if it had been every day. At least we would have known what to expect and had a routine to the chaos.

I remember being so humiliated when we were in public and my dad would drink too much. A few beers in, he would start slurring his words, and his mouth had no filter for what was appropriate. Even when my dad is sober, he tends to be a person without much regard for people's feelings. He will tell you exactly what he thinks of you whether it hurts your feelings or not. Imagine that after a few beers, and you can see why so much of my childhood I dreaded going anywhere with him where there would be alcohol, and I knew he would embarrass us with his snide comments to other people.

My dad is Polish, and his family is mostly Catholic, so he has a very large extended family. A big family means lots of big wedding celebrations, and most of the time at a Catholic wedding dance, there is going to be plenty of alcohol. I always looked forward to seeing cousins and dancing at the weddings, but I also dreaded them. I knew that my dad was going to drink too much. So the evenings always started out fun, but that changed quickly when I could see that he was intoxicated and starting to slur his words. It was so embarrassing listening to him talk to people with slurred speech and inappropriately flirt with women right in front of my mom. He would always pick a cute, skinny blonde to dance with instead of my mom. I always wished I was blonde because it was very clear that my dad found blondes attractive. I never remember my mom being jealous of him dancing with other women, but I think she was maybe relieved that she didn't have to dance with him when he was drunk. The night normally ended with my mom driving us home and crying silently to herself so my brother and I wouldn't know, but I always knew. It was the worst when my dad would have to sit in the back seat with us because we gave my grandpa a ride to the wedding, and he would sit in the front seat. My dad would pass out in the middle of us in the back seat and be snoring on us. I would try to sit on the floor so

I didn't have to smell the strong stench of alcohol or be squashed by him.

His drinking was the source of many, many tears for my mom and me when I was growing up, less for my brother because he wanted to appear tough. He expressed his anger toward my dad in other ways, like smashing his bottles of alcohol in front of his shop door. We never talked about our feelings to my dad. I would cry to my mom about it and cry when I saw her sad, but we never really learned how to communicate. After one of my dad's benders, my mom would always ignore him for a few days or weeks, depending on how bad it had been; then she would end up feeling guilty for being mad and act like everything was normal. He would get drunk again, and the vicious cycle would continue.

I tried to express my hurts to my dad a couple of times in letters. I know that he read them, but he never spoke a word about them to me. I'm not sure if they tugged at his heartstrings at all or not, but I poured my innocent, child heart out to him in those letters. I told him about how much it hurt me when he would drink and how much it hurt me and my mom when he would say mean things to her, but my feelings were never acknowledged. I don't know if he ever felt bad about what he was doing to his family or not.

I am grateful that my father was never physically abusive to us when he would drink. I know there are so many families that deal not only with a father who is an alcoholic but also with one who hurts them physically. The hurts caused by my father were mostly from his words. Many of them I will remember for the rest of my life. I think it hurt me more hearing the hurtful comments toward my mom than the comments directed at me. When my dad drank, he always made comments about my mom's weight. She has never been a "skinny" woman, even before she had kids, but she has always been beautiful both inside and out. She had big babies; I weighed over nine pounds when I was born, and my beast of a brother weighed in at twelve pounds one-half ounce. I also need to mention she had us naturally—yes, naturally. For all the mamas reading this, we know that after that, your body will never be the same. Some men cherish the changes in their wives' bodies because of the blessing of their children, but that was not the case for my dad. A woman's worth came from the way she looked and the way she cooked.

I remember from the time I was six years old being concerned with my weight and thinking I was "fat." Hearing my dad tell my mom she was overweight made me think that my worth came from what I looked like at a very young age. I wasn't overweight as a child by any means, but my two best friends at school were very thin little girls. I always thought I was fat because my thighs looked bigger than theirs, and my wrists were nearly twice the size of theirs—being a big-boned Polish girl. I would put myself on diets without my mom knowing and was always concerned that I was fat.

From a young age, I thought that the only worth I would have to a man was in the way I looked. I will never forget a specific day when I was four years old. It was the first time I remember looking to my daddy for approval in the way I looked. It was 1987, right smack in the middle of the "big hair" trend of the '80s. I admired the teenage girls with their six-inch-high bangs and asked my mom if she could fix mine like that. So without making me look age-inappropriate, she ratted my bangs a little; I felt so cool and grown up. I looked like the big girls, and it was the first time I remember really feeling proud of the way I looked. I wanted to show off how pretty I looked, so I went to the place most little girls would go for words of affirmation—my dad. I remember going into the living room hoping to hear words of admiration, but his response was "Why would you do that to your hair?" I was completely crushed and embarrassed that I thought I looked cute. I wanted to run back into the bathroom and comb my bangs into the straight style they were normally in. I didn't say a word but avoided him for the rest of the day, feeling humiliated. I never remember looking to my dad for approval again because I knew I wasn't going to get it.

So from a young age, I turned to boys for approval and to feel pretty. As women, we have a need to feel loved and beautiful. As little girls, we look to our daddies for that love and approval. Sadly, so many girls like myself don't get the attention they need from their fathers, so they look to young men for it. I didn't realize until I was almost thirty years old that although my father wasn't able to give me the love and affection I needed because of his brokenness, I have a Heavenly Father who can. I am hoping that by reading this book, you will be able to understand that you too have a Heavenly Father who loves you more than you can imagine and He can be the Daddy you have always longed for.

Did you know that you have a Heavenly Father who delights in you? A Heavenly Father who can save you? A Heavenly Father who loves you so much he sings over you? If you are like me, this was hard to imagine at first, but He says so in His Word.

> The LORD your God is with you, He is mighty to save. He will take great delight in you, He will quiet you with His love, He will rejoice over you with singing. (Zephaniah 3:17)

I want you to ponder these words for a moment and bask in the love your Heavenly Daddy has for you. Every minute of every day, He is drawing us nearer to Him, desiring a deeper relationship with us.

> I have loved you with an everlasting love; therefore I have drawn you with loving-kindness. (Jeremiah 31:3)

God loves us with an everlasting love. His love is not limited by humanness; it is absolutely unconditional and never ends. He loves you and He loves me. Period. No strings attached.

Our Family Brokenness

We are living in a broken world, but this isn't the way God created the world to be. In the beginning, there was no sin. Adam and Eve lived in the Garden of Eden and enjoyed living in unrestricted fellowship with God. God actually walked and talked with Adam and Eve in the garden. How amazing is that?

God gave Adam and Eve everything they needed. Their lives were beautiful and carefree. They had only one rule to obey in the garden. God told Adam, "You are free to eat from any tree in the garden; but you must not eat from the tree of the knowledge of good and evil, for when you eat of it you will surely die" (Genesis 2:16–17).

This seems so simple. Just stay away from the tree, and you will continue to live the good life. As we read Genesis 3, we see how Satan deceives Eve and makes the tree look so inviting, so tempting. She is the first to be betrayed by the Evil One who comes only to steal and kill and destroy (John 10:10).

> Now the serpent was more crafty than any of the wild animals the LORD God had made. He said to the woman, "Did God really say, 'You must not eat from any tree in the garden'?" The woman said to the serpent, "We may eat fruit from the trees in the garden, but God did say, 'You must not eat fruit from the tree that is in the middle of the garden, and you must not touch it, or you will die.'" "You will not certainly die," the serpent said to the woman. "For God knows that when you eat from it your eyes will be opened, and you will be like God, knowing good and evil." When

the woman saw that the fruit of the tree was good for food and pleasing to the eye, and also desirable for gaining wisdom, she took some and ate it. She also gave some to her husband, who was with her, and he ate it. Then the eyes of both of them were opened, and they realized they were naked; so they sewed fig leaves together and made coverings for themselves. Then the man and his wife heard the sound of the LORD God as he was walking in the garden in the cool of the day, and they hid from the LORD God among the trees of the garden. But the LORD God called to the man, "Where are you?" He answered, "I heard you in the garden, and I was afraid because I was naked; so I hid."

And he said, "Who told you that you were naked? Have you eaten from the tree that I commanded you not to eat from?"

The man said, "The woman you put here with me—she gave me some fruit from the tree, and I ate it."

Then the LORD God said to the woman, "What is this you have done?"

The woman said, "The serpent deceived me, and I ate."

So the LORD God said to the serpent, "Because you have done this,

"Cursed are you above all livestock and all wild animals! You will crawl on your belly and you will eat dust all the days of your life.

And I will put enmity between you and the woman, and between your offspring and hers; he will crush your head, and you will strike his heel."

To the woman he said,

"I will make your pains in childbearing very severe; with painful labor you will give birth to children. Your desire will be for your husband, and he will rule over you."

To Adam he said, "Because you listened to your wife and ate fruit from the tree about which I commanded you, 'You must not eat from it,'

"Cursed is the ground because of you; through painful toil you will eat food from it all the days of your life. It will produce thorns and thistles for you, and you will eat the plants of the field. By the sweat of your brow you will eat your food until you return to the ground, since from it you were taken; for dust you are and to dust you will return."

Adam named his wife Eve, because she would become the mother of all the living.

The LORD God made garments of skin for Adam and his wife and clothed them. And the LORD God said, "The man has now become like one of us, knowing good and evil. He must not be allowed to reach out his hand and take also from the tree of life and eat, and live forever." So the LORD God banished him from the Garden of Eden to work the ground from which he had been taken. After he drove the man out, he placed on the east side of the Garden of Eden cherubim and a flaming sword flashing back and forth to guard the way to the tree of life." (Genesis 3:1-24 NIV)

And the brokenness and pain of this world began...

Satan didn't stop with Adam and Eve. He seeks to deceive and devour each and every one of us. He specializes in tearing apart families and causing hurt and brokenness from generation to generation.

My father is a product of the brokenness in his family, and his father a product of the brokenness in his. I pity my dad because I believe the way he treated my mom and his alcoholism was a result of what he grew up seeing. My grandfather was an alcoholic and did not treat my grandmother very well. From the stories I have heard, my grandmother lived with a lot of turmoil from her marriage and cried a lot just like my mom did. She died when my dad was only seventeen years old. I never met her, but she sounds like a wonderful woman; I would have loved to know my grandma. I think she probably had a lot of the same qualities that my mom does.

From what I remember of my grandfather, he was a hard man. By the time I was old enough to remember, he had quit drinking but still wasn't the joyful grandpa type. He didn't say a lot, but if he didn't like someone or something they were doing, he definitely wasn't afraid to tell them. As he aged, he softened a little; and by the time he was in a nursing home the last few years of his life, I learned to appreciate my grandpa. I also felt sorry for him because he harbored so much bitterness toward people he didn't like and just couldn't let it go.

We are all products of what we grew up with, good or bad. Sometimes we choose to follow the unhealthy patterns of our parents, and in other situations, we choose to make better choices for our lives and learn from the mistakes of our parents. My dad chose to follow the example he was given. As a result, our family was very unhealthy and damaged.

I became bitter and angry toward my dad at a young age. I hated him for choosing alcohol over his family. I would beg him to stop drinking with words and letters. I couldn't understand why alcohol was more important than me, my mom, and my brother. I hated the way he treated my mom and felt a constant burden to try to protect her from more hurt. She was such a loving mom, always trying to do the best for us even though she was in a lonely marriage and very bitter toward her husband. As a little girl, I wondered when my parents would get a divorce. I never saw them say loving and kind words to each other. I remember wishing my mom would leave and find someone who would treat her nicely—the way I thought she deserved to be treated.

Looking back, I truly believe that my dad loved my mom in the only way he knew how—the only way he was taught to love a woman. He loved having her there to cook, clean, and care for his children. He loved the idea of a wife but didn't know how to show her love. He didn't know what a loving marriage was because he didn't see an example of one growing up. He wasn't following Christ and leading his family the way God intends for a man to lead his family. He didn't know Jesus personally and didn't have Christ's love overflowing from his heart into his family. He was doing life, marriage, and parenting the only way he knew how.

I am thankful God is breaking that pattern for my family, thankful that He is teaching my husband and me how to have a more loving marriage than I saw growing up. Teaching us how to raise our children to love Him and live their lives for Him. He is changing the brokenness for my family, and He can do it for yours as well!

My Younger Years

I was born on a small farm in northwest Minnesota. When I was three years old, my dad moved our family to the Twin Cities for reasons I will never understand. I hated living in a city. I loved animals and farm life and wished that we could move back "up north" so that I could live close to my grandma and have our horses on our own property.

The summer I turned twelve, my dream came true. The day school ended for the year; we moved back to our farm in northwest Minnesota, and I was able to have my first dog, raise rabbits, and have more horses than we were able to have when we had to board them in the city. It was the best summer I had ever had. I was so happy to be with my animals; they gave me purpose and showed me love.

My dad's drinking increased when we moved because he was back home with old buddies and could drink and drive more easily without getting caught in a rural area. I tried to ignore it and be happy with my animals, but everything changed when school started in the fall. It was awful. The girls in my sixth-grade class were so mean to me. I was very shy and self-conscious, and the girls didn't like me because I was the new girl, or maybe they were jealous. I will probably never know the motives behind their hate for me, but it made school a terrible place to be. I cried myself to sleep every night, praying that God would make it so I didn't have to go to school. I just wanted to fit in and be popular.

I still remember my sixth-grade year and the dread of going to school like it was yesterday, but today, I can thank God for that experience. I have such a heart for young girls who feel like they are unworthy because of the way they are treated by their peers. I have been able to speak into the lives of girls who are experiencing what I did when I was young and have been able to share the love of Christ with them. I am so thankful that God can take negative experiences in our lives and use them to help others and to glorify Him.

By eighth grade, the girls were nicer, and school was getting better, but I struggled a lot with self-image. I looked for attention from boys to try to fill the void of not having a relationship with my dad. I latched on to the high school basketball star who was two grades older than me because it made me feel special that he liked me. I finally felt accepted and popular.

I hated my dad for his drinking and smoking so much that I was never going to drink or smoke. I wanted so badly to fit in and be "cool" that I started drinking and partying in high school. I also started smoking because my boyfriend and his friends did, and I didn't want to look like the "good little church girl" that peers teased me about.

I was diligent in school and got good grades even though some of my choices outside of school weren't good. I hoped my dad would praise me when I brought home report cards with A's, but normally, I just got a "good job" comment, and he didn't seem interested in looking at it. I excelled at distance running and was in track and cross-country through ninth grade. Although I was placing at every meet, I quit because I wasn't being encouraged in it. My dad didn't come to my meets because they were boring and weren't worth his time, but when my brother started playing basketball, he went to most of his games because he liked watching basketball. I worked hard on our farm cleaning barn, keeping our horse tack organized, working with the horses, and anything I could do to try to make my dad happy. I was constantly striving to earn my worth.

My dad has a shingling business, and I worked for him during summer vacations for about ten years of my life. My dad is a very hardworking man, and I appreciate the importance of good work ethic that he taught us. I worked extremely hard and tried to do everything just right to try to earn his favor. I wore out my young body tearing off shingles in the summer heat to try to impress him. I tried to finish all my tasks just right so that he would be proud of a job I did. I still never seemed to do it right. If I went down the ladder for some reason, I should have known what to bring him when I came back up instead of coming up empty handed. If I was told to get something, I should have known to grab something he forgot to tell me as well.

I felt like I couldn't do anything right for him. I would hear people say, "Is that your daughter? Wow, she works really hard." Although it was nice to hear people admire my work ethic, I just wanted to hear it from my dad. Once, when he didn't realize I could hear, I overheard him telling someone what a hard worker I was. He said I could tear off shingles faster than most of the guys he had ever hired! Yep, he said it, and I heard it! He did think I was a hard worker, and my efforts to impress him were paying off! But why, why couldn't he just tell me? Why couldn't he have told me to my face that he was proud of me and that I was doing a good job? I probably will never know the answer. For some reason, in his brokenness, he could not express in words the things I needed to hear. He could not show me love the way I wish he could have.

*****

The summer before my senior year, I went to a youth convention in Estes Park, Colorado. I went to the altar call they had at one evening service. I wanted to make changes and start living the way God wanted me to. I was so excited about starting new, but it was hard to follow the right path and change when you still have the same friends and influences. I had no idea how to live life as a follower of Christ and had no one mentoring me. My parents took me to church, but they did not know what it was to live your life for Christ. They believed if you were baptized, confirmed, and believed in God, you were going to heaven; and there was nothing more to it—so there was no God in our home. We prayed a memorized prayer at meals, but other than that, God was not talked about, and we didn't pray together or read the Bible together.

I wanted to be different, but I also didn't want to be become unpopular again as I had strived so hard to reach popularity. I felt like I was riding the fence. I was still dating my first boyfriend, and although I wanted to make changes in my life, I wasn't willing to give anything up in order to let God run my life. I wasn't willing, and I didn't know how.

When you make that step to follow Christ, you absolutely have to be willing to let go of the negative influences in your life. They may be friends you have had all your life or they may be family members or it might be a job or hobby that you need to let go. The hard truth is we have to be willing to separate ourselves from the world, or we get pulled right back into the same things we have always done. I wish I could say that after that altar call, my life was changed and I followed Christ and led my family and friends to Him, but that wasn't the case. I was sucked right back into the patterns of the world because that was my comfort zone. I wasn't willing to give up the popularity I had been striving for and didn't want people to think I was weird.

Today, I don't care anymore. I know people are watching, critiquing, and analyzing my life, wondering why I'm so weird, wondering why I don't do the worldly things I used to do.

If we are born again, God expects our lives to be so different from that of the world that we would be considered weird, "a peculiar people."

> But ye are a chosen generation, a royal priesthood,
> a holy nation, a peculiar people;
> that ye should shew forth the praises of him who
> hath called you
> out of darkness and into his marvelous light.
> (1 Peter 2:9 NKJV)

Being a peculiar people isn't easy. I have never been someone who wanted to put myself out there and do something different that might make me stand out or that I may be ridiculed for. But when we make that decision for Christ, we have to be willing to die to ourselves, take up our cross, and follow Him.

> Then Jesus said to his disciples, "Whoever wants
> to be my disciple must deny themselves and take
> up their cross and follow me." (Matthew 16:24)

When I went to the altar call that night, the Holy Spirit was prompting me, and I wanted to follow Him, but I let the world pull me back in. My flesh was weak, and I didn't know how to follow Christ and wasn't completely ready either. So I spent many more years trying to fill that void in my life with worldly things. Instead of taking up my cross when I went back school that fall for my senior year, I chose to follow the way of the world. I achieved my goal of being popular and was crowned homecoming queen. Although I was considered one of the most popular girls at school, I still felt empty.

My friend, I pray that you would not spend years wasting time on earthly pleasures like I did. Don't wait years to change your life because you are afraid of what people will think and afraid you will lose friends. God will replace those friends with friends who will help you in your walk with Him rather than hinder it. Will it be easy? No! Will people think you are weird? Of course! Is it worth it? Absolutely! God loves you so much that He sent His son to die for you! He was willing to do that for you. Isn't it worth giving your life to Him?

> For God so loved the world that he gave his one
> and only Son,
> that whoever believes in him shall not perish but
> have eternal life. (John 3:16)

*****

Years later, when I was struggling in a marriage, my mom sought help from a local pastor who is now a good family friend. He prayed over me one evening without knowing anything about my past or much about what I was going through at the time. He prayed that I would know how much my Heavenly Daddy loves me and that I would run to His embrace and feel His great love for me. I sobbed and sobbed that night realizing for the first time that even though

23

I didn't feel like I was loved by my earthly daddy, I had a Daddy in heaven who loved me. I had always thought of God as a faraway being, untouchable and unrelatable, but that night I learned that He is warm and loving—everything you could ever want in an earthly daddy and so much more. I wish I had grasped this concept when I was that teenage girl struggling to fit in and feel loved. My Heavenly Daddy was watching me and loving me and patiently waiting to have a relationship with me.

I pray that you, dear friend, would know without a doubt that God loves you more than you can imagine. He is your Heavenly Daddy, and just like He was waiting patiently for me to come to Him, He is also waiting for you. Let this be the day that you surrender to the greatness of His love and run into His loving embrace.

My Friend Zip

Throughout high school, horses were often my refuge. My parents raised registered quarter horses and paints. With my passion for horses, my life would have been a dream come true if there hadn't been so much dysfunction in my family. I loved working with horses and trained my first horse when I was fourteen years old. It was a horse named Zip. The ironic thing is Zip was a gift from my father.

Zip was what most horse breeders would call an accident. His mother, Zippos Girl Ginger, was purchased to be a broodmare. Being it was late summer when she was purchased, she wouldn't be bred until the following spring. Well, sometimes animals have other ideas. Ginger found her way in with our stallion one night and ended up being bred in the month of October—definitely not a month that any wise horse breeder would choose to breed a mare.

The following September, the most adorable sorrel colt was born to Ginger. He had a wide blaze on his face, hind socks, and one white spot on his left knee. He was as cute as can be! I fell in love with him immediately. He was kept in my grandpa's barn at the next farm over for the winter. The large empty barn provided a lot of space for the colt and his mama to stay warm during the cold months. I went over to visit him almost daily and gave him the barn name Zip. I became very attached to the little "accident" and started planning and saving to buy him from my parents.

On Christmas that year, after all the gifts had been opened, a lone card remained under the tree. My name was on the envelope in my dad's handwriting. I tried not to show my anxiety as I opened the card. It was a printed Christmas card. On the inside, underneath the greeting, read, "Zip is yours. Take good care of him. Love, Dad."

I couldn't believe it. This colt who began his life as an accident, whom I had grown to love, was mine! Looking back, I know this was my dad showing me he loved me in the only way he knew how. Without knowing it, my dad also had provided a way for me to cope with the things I was going through at home and being a teenager.

Zip wasn't a mistake after all. I believe God orchestrated that little "accident" into His grand plan. I will be forever grateful for the gift of Zip and all that he has taught me as well as the blessing he has been to others at our ranch.

I spent a lot of time with Zip as a teenager and fell in love with training horses after training him. I started training for customers during my summer vacations. I ended up selling Zip when he was four years old so I could buy a car. With many tears shed saying goodbye, I promised Zip that I would own him again one day.

After having a few different owners over the years, Zip now resides back on our ranch (the farm that belonged to my grandfather, where my dad grew up and where Zip spent his first winter in the big barn with his mama and where I live with my family). Zip will live out his remaining years on our ranch, being a blessing to the kids who come here for horse therapy.

The Rebellion Continues

I went on to college after I graduated high school and loved being free. I missed my mom but was also so relieved to not have to live by her rules and curfew anymore. During my high school years, my mom tried desperately to control my brother and me to keep us from making bad choices. She loved us so much and was doing the best she could parenting on her own because my dad didn't have much input. She would tell us that we shouldn't drink, do drugs, have sex, etc., because God didn't want us to.

As teenagers, we didn't really care. We didn't understand a relationship with Christ and the fact that living for Him brings more joy and peace than any drink or relationship ever could. In recent conversations with my mom, I have told her that I wish she would have shared more of her story with me when I was a teenager. I grew up thinking that my mom had been perfect when she was a teenager because she led me to believe that. I know she was trying to protect me and trying to keep me from making the same mistakes that she did when she was younger. She understands now that sharing her experiences with me and being honest with me would have spoken great volumes to me as a teenage girl. This is why I choose to tell my story, and when the time comes, I will share it with my children so they can learn from my mistakes in life.

When I was younger, I was tired of "Christians" pretending they had never messed up in their lives. I believed in God, but I didn't want to be a real "Christian" because I could never measure up. All the people who I thought were probably these true "Christians" appeared to have lived perfect lives, and I knew with the mistakes I had made, I could never compete with them. I hope that by sharing my story, those who feel unworthy of Christ's love and forgiveness will look at my mess of a life and realize that He really does rescue us from the darkness in our lives and forgive us our sins if we are truly repentant (Colossians 1:13–14).

I broke up with my high school boyfriend after my first semester of college but continued to make bad choices. I partied and dated a lot throughout college—still feeling very insecure and just wanting to feel loved and fill a void in my life.

Before my final two years of college, I decided to transfer to the University of Minnesota, Crookston. The college I was attending was in River Falls, Wisconsin, and I was very homesick. I missed my mom so much and knew it was really hard on her having both of her kids away at college. She was in a lonely marriage, and her kids were her life. I knew it broke her heart that we were gone, and I cried every time I had to leave to go back to Wisconsin.

I ended up living on my grandpa's farm, which was next to the farm my parents lived on. My grandpa hadn't lived there for a few years because he was in a nursing home, and I was excited to bring life to Grandpa's farm again. I later purchased it from my parents. It was the perfect place to set up my horse training facility. I was so happy that my life was finally falling into place. After completing my degree in equine science, I trained horses spring through fall and worked for a veterinarian in the winter months when it was too cold to train.

My life was going exactly as I wanted, but I was still feeling empty, still feeling like I would never be able to make my dad happy. He would make comments like "You will never make it training horses. Why didn't you become a nurse?" There was a constant void in my life that I was still trying to fill with partying and boyfriends. I would date guys because I wanted to feel loved, yet when I felt someone was getting too close to me and maybe falling in love with me, I pushed them away. I was afraid of getting hurt, and I didn't know how to have an intimate relationship. Physically, I gave myself to boyfriends because I felt like they would love me, but I didn't really want to totally commit to them. It left me feeling dirty, and I still didn't feel loved in the way I was longing for. I ended up getting married for the first time when I was twenty-seven years old. It was a marriage that brought me to my final fall.

My Final Fall

A year prior to my first marriage, I reached a very low point in my life when my mom and dad separated. My mom stayed in the marriage for twenty-eight years. I don't know how she managed, but she did. She always put on her happy face and was kind to those around her even though she was physically ill with ulcers and stomach pain from being in such an unhealthy situation. After she left, she felt like she could never be forgiven. She knew that God's desire isn't for a marriage to end. It took quite a few years before my mom realized who she is in Christ. Although she messed up and married a twenty-nine-year-old man without seeking the Lord's direction when she was only eighteen years old, and then walked away from the marriage years later, God forgave her. He forgave her not because she deserved to be forgiven, because none of us deserve forgiveness. He forgave her because He loves her, and she truly repented of her sin. It is only by the grace of God and a truly repentant heart that God can forgive our mistakes and make us new.

> Repent, then, and turn to God,
> so that your sins may be wiped out,
> that times of refreshing may come from the Lord.
> (Acts 3:19)

Even though my dad and I never really had a relationship to begin with, he blamed me for my mom leaving because I wouldn't tell her to go back. He completely cut ties with me and didn't speak to me for months. I remember being so depressed that I didn't want to get out of bed. I wanted to crawl in a hole and die.

I had spent twenty-six years of my life seeking approval and love from a father who was in so much bondage he couldn't give it and now was *totally* abandoned by him. It was devastating. I stayed home alone a lot during this time. Once in a while I would go out and try to find some fun in life, but it always left me feeling depressed and empty.

It was during this low point in my life that I met a guy who seemed to be just what I needed. He was smooth talking and told me just what I wanted to hear. He was also a very broken person in need of Jesus.

I became attached very quickly because I was lonely and vulnerable. I tried to overlook the fact that he drank too much, but I had enough after a few months of it. I didn't want to end up with someone like my dad. I saw some behaviors that concerned me when he drank, and I broke things off. Then he went back to South Dakota where he was from, and his parents put him in a thirty-day treatment center for his alcoholism. He called me almost daily while in treatment and shared with me how much I meant to him and how he thought he could change with God's help.

At this point in my life, I really wanted to change. I started Bible study with two women who were great mentors to me and spoke truth into my life. I will be forever grateful for these two friends in Christ who took the time to show me what a walk with Him looks like. It was then that I really started seeking the Lord's will for my life. I stopped drinking and partying completely and told the guy I was dating that I wouldn't be with someone who was going to make it hard for me to seek the Lord. He made me believe that God was changing him while in treatment. Now I realize it was just a way to manipulate and keep me.

When he finished treatment, he moved back to Minnesota, and we continued our relationship. He came to church with me and acted like he was trying to live for the Lord. A few months later, he proposed, and I said yes. He was going to AA meetings while we were engaged and seemed to be staying on track. Although he had stopped drinking, there were many behaviors that were red flags as well as a lot of jealousy. He would get very angry about small things, and the anger would turn to complete rage. The first big rage I saw him in after he quit drinking was a couple of weeks before our wedding. He broke the pantry door in my kitchen because he got upset about something. I confided in my mom about it because it really scared me. She said I could still back out of the wedding, but I was too embarrassed to call it off when the wedding was so close. How do you call five hundred people and tell them your wedding is off? Wow, would that have been a lot easier than what was to come! He was very jealous and controlling, but I hoped that would change once we were married.

It didn't change when we got married. It got worse.

There was so much craziness that went on in eleven months we lived together after our wedding that it seemed like I was living a Lifetime movie. It was horrible from day one. The day after we got married, we left for Minneapolis to catch a flight for a honeymoon in Jamaica. I remember crying on the way to the cities to leave for our honeymoon and asking God what I had gotten myself into. He got extremely upset with me and was going to leave me alongside the road. It all started because I asked if we could listen to the Christian music station. The honeymoon was awful, and he wanted to kick me out of our hotel room in Jamaica because he thought I was checking out black men. Let me remind you we were in Jamaica, and everywhere you look, there are men with dark skin.

He would get in rages once or twice a week and call me names almost daily. I was called every derogatory name you can think of and things I had never even heard of. The smallest things would set him off, such as asking him to take the garbage out, asking him to help me fix a fence, someone stopping over, a look he thought I gave someone, or a phone call from someone he didn't want me speaking to.

Almost every time he would get into a rage, he would finish screaming at me and throwing things; and then after he calmed down, he would sob and beg for forgiveness. He would tell me I didn't deserve to be treated like that and he would change, yet the pattern continued.

I didn't know what to do. I had never seen anyone act like this. I was embarrassed to tell anyone and felt very alone in the craziness. I would call my mom once in a while when it got really bad and I was afraid he would hurt me. Then I started hiding it from her too. He tried to isolate me from my mom, brother, friends, and anyone else I might have told about what he was doing.

I debated putting this part of my story in my book, but I felt it needed to be shared, not to condemn my ex-husband because he is a broken man who needs Jesus as much as all of us do, but to let other women who may be in similar situations know they are not alone. There are people who will help you and *believe* you! I honestly thought what I was going through only happened in movies. I didn't think real people acted that way. I was afraid that people would never believe my ex-husband did the things he did. After all, to other people he was charming, outgoing, funny, and a great guy. I was also embarrassed that I had gotten myself into the situation. I was afraid people would think I was stupid for marrying him and thought maybe it would be better just to deal with it rather than have people gossip about me. I live in a very small community in northwest Minnesota, and when there is juicy gossip, the whole town seems to know within days. I didn't want to be the talk of the town.

I pray that if you are in an unsafe relationship, you will not wait another day to seek help. Please do not ignore the warning signs like I did. Please do not believe that it will get better once you are married because it won't. If you are already married, please don't be afraid of what people will think. Please protect yourself and your children and seek help. There are people who will help you, and your Heavenly Father already knows you need help. Call out to Him and trust Him.

> Trust in the Lord with all your heart
> and lean not on your own
> understanding;
> in all your ways acknowledge him,
> and he will make your paths straight.
> (Proverbs 3:5–6)

If you know someone else who is in an unsafe relationship, I pray that you would not just listen to their stories but seek help with them. Let them know that you *believe* them and are there to help them, not condemn them. Encourage them to protect themselves and their children, and most of all, love them.

*****

I was dealing with all this craziness while pregnant. I became pregnant with my daughter two weeks after we were married and was devastated. It was already an awful situation, and I couldn't imagine bringing a baby into it. I remember wishing I would have a miscarriage because I didn't know how I could handle having a child in the situation.

My ex-husband was normally more verbally abusive than physically abusive. He would occasionally push me and hit me a couple of times, but most of the time he would scream at me and throw things around me. It got worse as each month went by. I was beginning to feel like I was the crazy one because he would blame me for all the things he was doing. The situation was spiraling out of control. Then the baby came.

Tyla Faith was born on September 18, 2011, and was the most perfect baby girl I had ever seen. Having an infant and being in an unstable relationship was very trying, and I prayed constantly that God would help us through our situation. When Tyla was about a month old, I was standing in our house holding her, and my ex-husband pushed me across the back. I fell, and her head was inches away from hitting a wooden bench in our house. At that point, I knew it wasn't just me that could get hurt anymore; it was my sweet baby girl. I prayed for protection for both of us but didn't know what else to do. About two weeks after that, he left me and went back to drinking and partying.

Although my husband had left me with a newborn, I felt like I couldn't get divorced. I had people telling me that if I trusted God, He would change him. Finally, after a couple of months of my ex partying and staying who knows where after the bars closed, I felt a peace about letting him go. I knew that God could change him, but

I also knew that God is a gentleman and doesn't make people change. My ex had to want to change and choose to follow Christ.

It was after he left that I really had to let go and leave things up to God. It was such a relief to have him gone but such a scary time as well. I didn't have to worry about myself anymore, but I had to worry about Tyla visiting him. I was terrified that she would have to be alone with him. I was bogged down with anxiety and worry to the point of having chest pains from the anxiety. I had never felt so out of control in my life, and that is exactly where God was able to reach me.

I was a single parent with a newborn—completely worn and exhausted. I was at the end of my rope. I had hit rock bottom, and that is where the Lord was able to meet me in my brokenness and change my heart. I remember sobbing on the kitchen floor one evening after putting Tyla to bed. I didn't think I could go on anymore and was praying for strength and forgiveness for all the awful things I had done in the past. I felt so dirty and unworthy of God's love.

It was that evening that I totally surrendered to my Heavenly Daddy who had been patiently waiting for me to give my life to Him. I was finally able to let go of all the awful things from my past and really felt like I was forgiven. I had been praying for forgiveness for the same things over and over again—my high school and college mistakes, as well as getting divorced. There were so many things I had done that broke God's heart. As I was praying and crying that night on my kitchen floor, I felt God saying to me, "Amanda, why do you keep asking Me to forgive you for the things I have already forgiven you for? I have forgotten about them, and you can too."

In Psalm 103:12, God says, "As far as the east is from the west, so far has he removed our transgressions from us." If we are truly repentant (meaning we completely turn away from the sin), God forgives us as far as the east is from the west!

Until that night, I had felt like such an awful person and so unworthy of forgiveness because I had made so many mistakes in my life. The past kept creeping up on me, and Satan kept reminding me of my mistakes, so I was unable to accept God's forgiveness and grace. It was so freeing to finally understand the concept of God's grace.

That night, I was made new in Christ, a new creation: "Therefore, if anyone is in Christ, he is a new creation; the old has gone, the new has come" (2 Corinthians 5:17). Was my life perfect after that night? No. I still live in a fallen world where I will have trials in this life. The difference is I have Christ to help me through, and I am made complete in Him. The emptiness I had felt my whole life was gone. The void I had been trying to fill with earthly pleasures was filled. My whole life I had been searching to fill the void of a broken relationship with my earthly father, not realizing that it could be filled with the love of my Heavenly Father—a love that doesn't change, no matter what. No matter if I'm popular or unpopular, fat or skinny, ugly or beautiful, successful in the world's eyes or a stay-at-home mom, He still loves me the same. Every single day. Period.

God's Great Grace

If the decision had been mine, I don't believe I would have ever chosen to have children. It is so funny when we try to make our own plans because God always has a way of changing our plans and hearts to fit into His plan.

> In his heart a man plans his course, but the Lord determines his steps. (Proverbs 16:9)

I can't imagine my life without my children and am so happy that God changed my plans for me. God used my precious baby girl to bring me to Him—a broken, desperate new mother, alone, crying out to my Father at the most trying time in my life. God and His great grace met me on the kitchen floor that night and changed my life for good. No more riding the fence. No more being a "Christian" around some people and not around others. I was all in, ready to follow Christ wherever He would lead me.

Surrendering your life to Christ doesn't mean it's going to be perfect, and it doesn't mean it's going to be easy. I do not ever want to give anyone the impression that because I am a follower of Christ, I am perfect. I am human and struggle daily. Just ask my kids or my husband if I am perfect, and they will tell you otherwise! I constantly need to be brought back to the cross and ask God to forgive me when I mess up. The difference is that when I choose to let God lead my life, He forgives me and sets me free: "So if the Son sets you free, you will be free indeed" (John 8:36).

God has blessed me so much more than I could have ever imagined when I finally surrendered. He has given me a heart for Him and a heart for young girls who are struggling with feeling unloved and empty. Working with youth, I have heard many stories from teenage girls who have had their hearts broken and stomped on by earthly fathers. In their hurt and brokenness, they say they cannot ever forgive their dads for abusing them or their mom or siblings, leaving their family, being an alcoholic or drug addict, and the list goes on and on. In our flesh, we cannot forgive the deepest hurts. We want to hate and hold on to the hurt. We want our fathers or anyone who has hurt us to hurt as much or more than we did. We cannot love them. Only by the grace of God and having a personal relationship with Jesus can we forgive those who have hurt us. We need to forgive them so that God can forgive us.

> For if you forgive men when they sin against you, your heavenly Father will also forgive you. But if you do not forgive men their sins, your Father will not forgive your sins. (Matthew 6:14–15)

We can even *love* those who have hurt us by the power of the Holy Spirit. That doesn't mean we need to have a relationship with them, or even like them. It is freeing ourselves from the burden of holding on to the sin of hate and unforgiveness. It is letting God deal with them and letting them go.

I can honestly say that I have been able to forgive my ex-husband and that I pray for him. Not in my own strength because my flesh wants to hold on to the bitterness of the hurts and betrayal. As God started healing me from my broken marriage, He blessed me beyond what I could have imagined. He put a godly man into my life who has shown me what it really means to love your family the way God intended a man to love his family.

I met my husband, Josh, about a year after I was divorced. I didn't feel worthy of such a kind man who had made better decisions in life than I had. I would ask him over and over again if he was sure he wanted to date me and live with all my past mistakes. He assured me that he did and he loved me in spite of my past, yet I struggled to believe him. When Josh and I were dating, I was attending a Mending the Soul group. It is for women who have been in abusive relationships of any kind and are seeking healing. It helps you understand the nature of abuse and helps you seek God's love and guidance on your healing journey. If you have been in an abusive situation, I would strongly recommend finding a Mending the Soul group in your area or read the book by Steven R. Tracy, *Mending the Soul: Understanding and Healing Abuse.*

I went home from a group meeting one night, and after I put my daughter to bed, I sat at the kitchen table and cried. We had been going through the part of the book on forgiveness, and although I knew I had already been forgiven of my past mistakes, I kept letting Satan tell me lies about myself. You are fat, you are ugly, you are unforgiven, you are a slut, you are stupid, you aren't good enough for Josh, and soon he will see that.

I got out a piece of paper that night and drew a large cross. On the cross, I wrote down all the negative words I had felt or was feeling about myself. Then, in large letters across the whole cross, I wrote FORGIVEN. A verse I wrote on the page read,

> Therefore, if anyone is in Christ,
> he is a new creation;
> the old has gone,
> the new has come. (2 Corinthians 5:17)

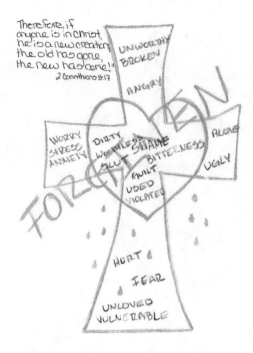

The next time I was able to talk to Josh in person, I timidly asked if I could show him something. I hated the thought of being vulnerable and talking to him about how I was feeling. After all, I had always been a tough cowgirl and was afraid of letting my guard down and telling him my feelings. I didn't know how to tear down the walls around my heart that had grown so hard and let him love me. I took out the cross I had made and explained how things in my past kept creeping up and making me feel unworthy. He listened and then assured me that he didn't think those things about me and that God didn't either.

The next time I saw Josh, he brought me a sheet of paper with a cross drawn on it similar to the one I had made. Instead of the ugly words that were written on my cross, his was filled with all the things he loved about me—beautiful, talented, intelligent, kind, strong, and so many more things that I have trouble believing about myself.

No man had ever said such beautiful words about or to me. Some of them were words I had longed to hear from my daddy as a little girl. Words that Josh truly meant about me. I tried to keep my tough image and not cry when I read the words, but the tears came. God had put a man in my life who loved Him and loved me. What a blessing!

*****

Josh and I were married when Tyla was two years old. We had no idea where her biological father was; but about a month after we were married, he called, said he heard I got married, and asked if Josh would adopt Tyla. I had been so worried about Tyla eventually seeing him, and just like that, he called and offered adoption. God is so good! It was such a blessing for us, and I know that God was protecting her. That call also broke my heart for him. He is so lost and in so much bondage that he doesn't even know what he is missing by giving up a child. Tyla has a smile that lights up her whole face. She is tiny in stature but fierce in personality. She is loving, caring, and kind and is always thinking about other people and what she can do for them. She is a precious daughter of our Heavenly Father and was adopted by my husband so that she can grow up knowing a loving earthly father.

*****

Josh and I both love the Lord and have a desire to live for Him. That said, you would assume our life together has been perfect, right? Wrong. Because of the brokenness in this world, we will all have trials. Josh and I have had a lot of ups and downs in our marriage.

We are both very strong-willed people and were thirty years old when we got married. We were both used to doing things the way we had always done them and didn't exactly want to change. We also started our marriage with a child, so we didn't get time to figure out marriage before having children. I was still healing from my past and hurts from my first marriage. Josh also had hurts and betrayal from his past that he was healing from. We were two broken people who loved each other and wanted to do our marriage God's way but have failed in so many ways. Although Josh knew about my past before we were married, as much as he wanted to be okay with it, at times he has still struggled with it. There are things from his past that I have struggled with as well.

Coming out of an abusive relationship, there were triggers that I would have if Josh did something that reminded me of my ex-husband. I would panic, and even if it were only for a moment, I would think he was going to behave the way my ex had.

The first time this happened was on our honeymoon. I was in the shower lost in thought and, with the loud fan, couldn't hear anything outside of the bathroom. Josh had been watching TV, and room service brought our food. He came into the bathroom to tell me, and I didn't hear him come in. He opened the shower curtain slightly, and the moment I saw it, I screamed and was brought back to an incident that had happened with my ex-husband. I was in the shower and didn't hear him come home from work. He came into the bathroom, tore down the cloth shower curtain, and started screaming at me, accusing me of being unfaithful—accusing his very pregnant wife of being unfaithful while he was at work because I was taking a shower at an odd time of the day. That day, I sat down and cried and cried in the shower wondering what I was going to do about my situation and what was going to happen once the baby came. On my honeymoon with Josh, I did the same thing. I told him I would be fine and sat in the shower and cried, wondering why I had to think of that incident on my honeymoon.

Josh and I were able to talk about it later, and he listened to me cry as I opened up about things that had happened in my first marriage. We prayed through it and enjoyed our honeymoon very much despite Satan putting thoughts in my head to try to sabotage it.

God didn't intend for us to go into marriage having to share things about our pasts with other people. God intended for "a man to leave his father and his mother and be united with his wife, and the two will become one flesh. So they are no longer two, but one flesh. Therefore what God has joined together, let no one separate" (Matthew 19:4–6). God didn't say leave his father and mother and be united with his wife and, when that doesn't work out, leave her and be united with another wife. God intended for us to get married and stay married. In our culture today, we are taught that marriage isn't that important and we should date a lot, sleep around, and try out marriage by living together before we are married. This is not at all the way God intended it to be, and it creates so much pain and jealousy in your future marriage. God intended one woman to be with one man, and that is when a marriage is its best. I hope that if you are not married, you would seek God's will for your future marriage and seek Him in making that decision. God knows that we live in a broken world, and we make mistakes. If you are like me and didn't listen to God's warnings before relationships and marriage, God offers you forgiveness and grace just like He did me. He can also help you to deal with the brokenness of your past so that it doesn't affect your future relationships. The only way Josh and I are able to deal with the struggles in our marriage is by clinging to our Redeemer and asking Him to guide us.

*****

We had a miscarriage a few months after we were married that was really hard on us. A few months later, I got pregnant again, and we were thrilled! Almost halfway into the pregnancy, I went in for a routine checkup; and when the doctor was listening for the baby's heartbeat, no heartbeat was found. The baby had died inside of me, and I had no idea. I had to come back to the hospital later that day and was given drugs to deliver our lifeless baby. It was a baby boy that his big sister named Thomas J. It was the most devastating thing Josh and I had ever gone through in each of our lives. We got to hold our precious son but would never hear him cry. We spent six hours with him, held him, and took pictures with him before he was taken to the funeral home.

Although it was the most devastating thing I have been through so far in my life, there was also a peace I had through it all. I knew my baby boy was with Jesus, and he would never have to know any pain in this world. He will only ever know love! I felt God's presence through the whole experience from the hospital room to the sadness in the days, weeks, and months after Thomas was born. Through the devastation of losing a baby, God gave me a heart for other women going through similar situations. I have been able to reach out to other women who have had miscarriages or lost their babies prior to birth. I have been able to weep with them and pray with them because I understand the hurt—a hurt you cannot imagine until you have been through it. It has also given me even more of a longing for heaven because I have two babies waiting for me there. What a glorious reunion it will be the day I go home to be with Jesus and can hold my two heavenly babies for the first time.

God healed our hearts over time, and although we will always love Thomas and wish he was with us on earth, we know we will see him in heaven. A year and a week after we lost Thomas, on December 17, 2015, our son, Jace Joshua, was born. I didn't know if I would even be able to carry a child full term after losing Thomas, so we were overjoyed and so thankful for our baby boy. He made our little family complete and brings so much joy to our lives.

I love Tyla and Jace so much and want them to have a different life than I did. I pray my kids will come to know and live for Jesus at a young age so they can avoid the mistakes I made growing up because I didn't know the Lord. I hope that they can learn from my mistakes so they don't have to go through the things I did. I am thankful they have a daddy who lets them know how much he loves them and also gives them a godly example of a husband and father.

*****

God has been with me every step of the way through my life. He was with the shy young girl who was so desperate to fit in and feel loved. He was with the young woman who made poor choices and was patient with her as she kept on making mistakes and walking further away from Him. He was with the newly married woman who knew she made a big mistake by not listening to His warning signs. He was with the single mother who was at the end of her rope and desperate for someone to rescue her.

He did just that. He rescued me from darkness and brought me into the light. Ephesians 5:8–10 reminds me so much of what God did in my life:

> For you were once darkness, but now you are light in the Lord. Live as children of light (for the fruit of the light consists in all goodness, righteousness and truth) and find out what pleases the Lord. Have nothing to do with the fruitless deeds of darkness, but rather expose them.

I am so thankful that even when I was rejecting Him, He was still drawing me to Himself. He was putting people in my life that spoke truth, even when I didn't want to hear it. He was paving the way to my salvation. I am not proud of the past I have, and it's not easy to expose the bad parts of your life to people; however, I know that God wants me to share the story of what He has done in my life, so I am choosing to obey.

A Letter from Mom

My Dearest Daughter,

Did you dream as I did when you were little of growing up and marrying Prince Charming and living happily ever after? I had a dream of marrying a cowboy, having two or three children, and having a horse ranch and a home for struggling kids. I got the cowboy, wonderful children, and some horses, but not the happily ever after.

As I read the book that you have written, the enemy wants to bring me back to a place of condemnation, a place of guilt and shame for the choices that I have made that had such big consequences, not only for me, but for you. The same mistakes I made were repeated by you, and I watched you hurt. I watched you struggle in bondage and did not know how to help you to be free—because I was not free. I let the enemy steal from me for so long. Just like you, from the very first day of marriage, I knew I had messed up. The sullen, moody man I had married struggled with alcoholism and his own set of bondage. He was not going to be the person that built me up, made me feel loved, and cherished or told me I was beautiful. Instead, I felt as if I were a possession, a maid. I was always waiting for the next negative mood swing and wondering what "I" did wrong. I struggled with feelings about my body image not being desirable, and those insecurities affected you.

Because of the patterns of dysfunction, I never respected your dad as the head of the home. He didn't lead us, and his words were so often hurtful. I didn't help your dad in his brokenness either, and he didn't feel loved. I felt angry inside about the things that went on, so I did not show you what God meant for a wife to be like toward her husband. I thought I was keeping those things well-hidden from

46

you. Now I know that you always knew, and you felt like you needed to fix things from a very young age.

Your brother had an ulcer at seven years old, and you were seeing a counselor at twelve. I didn't see that you just needed a truly peaceful home with Jesus Christ as the center. Your brother became the funny guy to smooth over situations and to cover up hurt. You, my precious daughter, became a perfectionist to try to measure up for never hearing the words "I love you" and being valued for who you were, not what you did.

I watched you make many of the same choices I did and marry a man who was deceptive and yet seemed so perfect because he knew just what to say. I watched you weep and feel so unloved and unworthy in an unsafe marriage, and no matter how much I loved you and told you that, you needed to be whole in Christ to feel that love. I watched your tortured ex-husband abuse his wife because he was such a mess inside. I cried out to God to rescue us, and He did, but there are consequences for sin, and we were reaping what we had sewn. God loves us so much that He allows those consequences to happen in order to teach us, to make us stronger and ultimately to bring us to the foot of the cross.

> If anyone wishes to come after Me,
> he must deny himself,
> and take up his cross daily and follow Me.
> (Luke 9:23)

Amanda, today I am so glad for your brokenness and mine, not because I wanted you to hurt but because it brought us to the end of ourselves, where Christ was able to reach us. It's amazing to watch God work when we turn our lives and wills over to Him. He can do a much better job at running our lives than we can if we let Him.

I will never forget the night I lay in bed in my apartment alone, a few months after leaving your dad. I cried out to God, "Lord, if You are really there, if You could possibly love me after the mess I have made of life, please, please forgive me and please let me feel Your presence. Oh how I need You!" I immediately felt the overwhelming feeling of being physically held in His arms. It is something that I cannot even describe to you. I was like a child in a parent's arms, enveloped in total peace.

> In the day when I cried out,
> You answered me,
> and made me bold with strength in my soul.
> (Psalm 138:3)

This is my prayer for you, Amanda: that you walk in your Father's ways, even though they are not always easy; that you feel His arms around you and His Spirit guiding you. I pray that you can leave the baggage in the past and walk in freedom from all the strongholds that the Enemy has tried to keep you in. I love you dearly, but that isn't enough. Your true value is found only in Jesus Christ. This life isn't a fairy tale; and the Enemy will continue to try to steal, kill, and destroy. He will continue to tell you lies and try to deceive you, but he will not have victory.

When I look at you today, Amanda, instead of a broken child, a broken woman, I see a new creation in Christ. Are you perfect? No. But you are striving to be a true follower of Christ. You have had to tear down walls brick by brick from the bondage of the past. I have watched you begin to trust. I have watched you become less defensive and strive to give up control. I have watched your decisions turn from self to selfless. I have watched you give up money and time to homeschool your children and bring them up with the Lord as the center of all. I have watched you learn to trust a Daddy that is beyond good and faithful, whose promises are true and whose love is beyond anything we can comprehend.

Can I ever begin to thank my Good, Good Father for what He has done for us? Will I ever lose my sense of joy and thankfulness when I listen to my grandchildren pray or sit in the back seat of my car and sing praises to Jesus at the top of their lungs? I hope not. I am so thankful that He brought us out of the darkness and into His wonderful light so that it can overflow into the lives of your children—my grandchildren.

The legacy that I want to leave for you, your brother, your spouses, and my grandchildren is the one that I began at forty-five years old. I wasted a whole lot of my life trying to make my own legacy, but I will strive to finish this race on the right track until the day He calls me home. My desire is to spend the rest of my days sowing seeds for Jesus into you, your family, and the world.

> Blessed is a man who perseveres under trial;
> for once he has been approved,
> he will receive the crown of life which the Lord
> has promised to those who love Him. (James 1:12)

I am proud of you for opening your heart to people through this book and being vulnerable and honest. I am praying that someone reading it might not waste another day in bondage to sin and the patterns of this world, that someone who feels useless and worthless might know that they have value to their Heavenly Father and they will cry out to Him for rescue.

> Come to me, all you who are weary and burdened,
> and I will give you rest.
> Take my yoke upon you and learn from me,
> for I am gentle and humble in heart,
> and you will find rest for your souls.
> For my yoke is easy and my burden is light.
> (Matthew 11:28–30)

My heart leaps for joy when I watch you care about the souls of others, Amanda. It costs us the world to follow Christ and be His disciple, but I am so thankful that you no longer want the empty things the world has to offer, but instead want to live a life that is holy and to be the hands and feet of Jesus. The narrow path has protection and peace for you, my daughter.

All my love,
Mom

Giving God Your Hurts and Anger

I think we often pretend that as followers of Christ, it is easy to be nice and loving to everyone. We put on a façade that we don't struggle with hateful thoughts about other people. Maybe some are afraid to be transparent and admit their struggles, but even as born-again Christians, we still stumble into sin. The difference is that instead of continuing in the sin and letting it take root and grow in our hearts, we take it to the cross and repent.

My hurts and anger toward my dad and my ex-husband didn't go away overnight just because I gave my life to Christ. Little by little, day by day, God is continuing to help me work through the hurts and pray blessings for those who have hurt me. Some days it's easier than others.

I believe God understands our anger, yet He doesn't want us to let our anger take a foothold and grow into bitterness and hate. He tells us to "take every thought captive to the obedience of Christ" (2 Corinthians 10:5). We can read in Luke 4 about how Jesus was tempted by Satan, but He did not give in to the temptation. Jesus even had righteous anger at times; as we read in Matthew 21 and Luke 19, Jesus was angry at the Pharisees because of their hard hearts. Yet in His anger, He did not sin.

When I was going through divorce, it was so hard not to absolutely hate my ex-husband and what he was doing. Some days this was an all-day struggle. Satan would keep putting negative thoughts in my head, and the things my ex did to me would keep flooding my mind. On those days, if I would submit myself to God and resist Satan, he would flee (James 4:7). When a hateful thought would come to mind, I needed to take it to Christ, repent of the hate in my heart, and pray for salvation and blessings for him.

The only way I could do this was by being in the Word even more and by praying without ceasing—praying for his salvation and blessings for him, praying for forgiveness for the hurtful things I said to him out of anger, praying that I can love him as a child of God and not hate him because of the things he did out of his own hurts and brokenness. Love doesn't mean accepting what he did as right. Love means loving him as Christ does even though he has made mistakes because I have also made mistakes, and God still loves me and forgives me if I ask Him to.

It is easier to be forgiving to my ex-husband than my dad because he is out of my life, and I never have to see him. I have forgiven him and given it to God to deal with him and pray that his heart will change one day. It isn't always as easy to be forgiving to my dad who still lives on the farm right next to me and my family.

After my mom left, it took months before my dad would speak to me; and even after he did start speaking to me again, it was clear that he still blamed me that my mom was gone. It is so easy for us to blame someone else instead of taking responsibility for our own actions. My dad was completely blind to the hurt my mom, his son, and his daughter experienced through the years; and I think he truly believed it couldn't have been anything he did. It had to be someone else's fault. If we look at our own lives, isn't this something we all do when we don't want to own up to the pain we have caused in other people's lives?

When I get into an argument with my husband, I immediately want to blame him and don't want to take responsibility for my part in the disagreement. Without the help of Christ, my selfish nature always wants to be the victim. With Christ, He is showing me how to take responsibility for my part and how to ask for forgiveness when I am wrong: "For all have sinned and fall short of the glory of God" (Romans 3:23).

Slowly, very slowly, I think my dad is beginning to see how his actions affected our family. I believe that he is trying to let go of the bitterness but still needs Jesus to set him free. Just as I didn't learn how to have a relationship with Jesus growing up, my dad didn't learn how to either. I continue to pray that he will let go and let

God into those bitter and angry areas of his life and be set free. I am looking forward to the day when my dad gives his life completely to Christ and is free of his bitterness and the hold alcohol has on his life. I am going to be rejoicing along with the angels when that day comes. And I truly believe it will.

The Power of Words

Beautiful words in a card from a friend can brighten someone's day. A heartfelt word spoken to someone who is hurting can help ease the pain. An encouraging word to a child can make them feel loved and special. Words are powerful, and just as easily as they can bring a smile to our face, a hurtful word has the power to destroy.

There are many places in the Bible where God addresses our words and how important it is to carefully choose our words.

> Do not let any unwholesome talk come out of
> your mouths,
> but only what is helpful for building others up
> according to their needs,
> that it may benefit those who listen. (Ephesians 4:29)

> With the tongue we praise our Lord and Father,
> and with it we curse men, who have been made
> in God's likeness.
> Out of the same mouth come praise and cursing.
> My brothers, this should not be. (James 4: 9–10)

The tongue is powerful, and with it we can make someone feel loved and special or break their spirit and devastate them.

I believe some people are affected by words more than others. When I first read the book *The 5 Love Languages* by Gary Chapman, I had never thought of the concept of having a love language before. In his book, he explains how to express love to your spouse the way they respond best by figuring out what their love language is. The neat thing is it works in all relationships, not just marriages. If we know the love language of our friends, parents, or children, we can show them we love them in a way that makes them *feel* loved. Out of the five languages—words of affirmation, acts of service, receiving gifts, quality time, and physical touch—mine is words of affirmation. Since my love language is words of affirmation, words affect me a lot. The unfortunate part is I remember the hurtful ones a lot more than I remember the kind ones.

When I was a child, I so desperately wanted to be told I was beautiful and precious, that I mattered to my earthly daddy, that no matter what happened he would always love me. The words I received instead told me that I wasn't good enough, that I would never measure up, that my interests weren't worth his time. I don't remember the spankings I got as a kid when I disobeyed, but I remember the hurtful words—the ones that tore me down instead of building me up.

As time went on, I kept on believing the lies that Satan told me through my dad's words, and I let them define me. I didn't have an identity in Christ, so I let those hurtful words define who Amanda was. When I was crying out to the Lord that night on my kitchen floor as a broken single mother, it was the beginning of my new identity—my identity in my Creator.

I love how Neil T. Anderson describes our transformation in his book *The Bondage Breaker*.

> When we are born again, God transfers us out of the kingdom of darkness and into the kingdom of His beloved Son. We are not in Adam; we are in Christ. We are new creations.
>
> But because we were spiritually separated from God when we were physically born, we learned to live independently from Him. Though we become new creations when we are born again, our minds are still conformed to the world. The process of being transformed into the image of God takes time.

Just as it takes time to be transformed into the image of God, it also takes time to heal from words that have hurt us. I still remember a lot of the negative words, and sometimes if I let them, they still hurt. But as I have been learning to find my identity in Christ, I am learning truth to replace the lies that were told to me.

- I am God's daughter. (John 1:12)
- I have been chosen by God and adopted as His child. (Ephesians 1:3–8)
- I am complete in Christ. (Colossians 2:9–10)
- I am God's workmanship. (Ephesians 2:10)
- God has amazing plans for me. (Jeremiah 29:11)
- God loves me with an everlasting love and draws me with loving-kindness. (Jeremiah 31:3)

And the list goes on and on and on!

Satan will use people to tell us lies. "God doesn't love you." "You were never good enough for your dad and never will be." "How can you be good enough for God?" "You are ugly." "You are stupid." "You are fat." When our minds are flooded with these lies, we need to take these thoughts captive to the obedience of Christ and remember who we are in Him. If the thought doesn't align with the Word of God, we know it isn't truth, and we shouldn't dwell on it. Instead, think about these things: "Whatever things are true, whatever things are noble, whatever things are just, whatever things are pure, whatever things are lovely, whatever things are of good report, if there is any virtue and there is anything praiseworthy—meditate on these things" (Philippians 4:8).

You are God's precious child, and He wants you to start believing His truth about you rather than what Satan and the world are telling you about yourself. When you are struggling with lies, grab a Bible and let God tell you what He thinks about you. Trust me, His words will change your life.

Sky

I have a mare called Sky that reminds me so much of myself. I purchased her nineteen years ago when she was just a yearling and I was seventeen years old. She has amazing cutting horse bloodlines and cost me all the hard-earned two thousand dollars I had to my name. I was the proud owner of a well-bred cutting horse and had a whole lot of work ahead. She hadn't been handled much her first year of life and was a challenge from the beginning.

When I brought her home, she would try to climb the walls of the box stall to get away from me. She even ended up in the hay manger one day as she panicked to try to get away. The fear in her eyes was so real. She thought with every ounce of her trembling body that I was going to hurt her. After a while, she learned to trust me a little. She learned that I wasn't going to hurt her, yet she still has never been a horse that wants to be around people, especially men. Most of our horses come when we call or stand at the fence when we are outside, hoping we will give them some attention or treats. Not Sky. When she was younger, it would sometimes take me close to an hour to catch her. I was late for a horse show more than once because she had other ideas.

By doing horse therapy at our ranch, I have learned so much about how horses often mirror people. As I look at my life and my relationships, it reminds me so much of the way Sky is with me. She is afraid of trusting me too much.

Even at twenty years old, she still eyes me coming with a halter, and I can tell by her body language that she is wondering how she can sneak away. Even when I go out to the pasture just to check on the horses, she watches the other horses come to be petted; and she stands off to the side, watching, but always keeping me at arm's length, never desiring me to be too close. When we are at a horse show, she runs her heart out for me and has earned many trophies over the years. We have made a great team, yet she still doesn't seem to trust me 100 percent. She has been with me much longer than the most important people in my life, my husband and my children, and she *still* doesn't want to be close to me!

So often in my life I have felt like Sky, not trusting people and not wanting to let them get too close to me—especially men, afraid they will hurt me like my dad or other men I've had relationships with.

There is a man who is a friend and godly mentor to Josh and me. When I first met this man, he taught the adult Sunday school class at our church. He was the same age as my dad and even somewhat resembled my dad in looks and stature. Whenever he would lead the class, I would put up a wall and tune him out. Although he was speaking truth to us, I couldn't hear it because he reminded me so much of my dad.

As time went on, I got to know him a little better and heard his testimony on a Sunday when he spoke for our pastor who was gone. When I saw that he was speaking that day, I wanted to leave. I sat in the pew, looking like I was paying attention but with the intent of not listening to a word he had to say. When he started to share how he was abused by his earthly father as a child, I began to listen. This was the first time I listened to what this man had to say. Although I hadn't been physically abused by my father, I too had deep hurt from my childhood and could relate. When I stopped letting this man remind me of my father, I was able to learn so much from him and his journey of forgiveness. I was able to learn to trust someone who had reminded me so much of my dad and build a relationship with him.

My issues with trust have affected my marriage too. I often remind myself of Sky in my relationship with Josh. I am afraid of letting my walls down and being vulnerable with him—afraid of getting hurt. Even though I know he is different than my dad and my ex-husband, I still try to keep him at arm's length. Although he showers me with affection and compliments like I shower Sky with kindness and treats, I have a hard time letting him love me, just like she has a hard time letting me love her. After almost twenty years together, Sky does her job for me and gives me 100 percent every time, but she still won't let me love her.

God has been showing me how much I have been like Sky in my marriage. I don't want to spend my life "stuck" like her. I don't want to spend the next twenty years of my marriage keeping my husband at arm's length. Slowly, God has been showing me how to let Josh love me, how to believe his affection is loving and true, and how to believe his compliments are what he really thinks of me. God is showing me what a beautiful thing my marriage can be if I let go and be loved.

Scars

We all want to be healed and free from the scars of our lives, right? It isn't always easy to let God heal us. We get used to the unhealthy patterns in our lives, and we feel comfortable stuck in the strongholds.

There are times when it is really hard not to be bitter or angry at the people who have hurt us, especially if we still have a relationship with them. Recently, I saw the dad of a friend of mine who is a very sweet and kind man and about the same age as my dad. He told me that I get prettier every time he sees me! What a compliment for a thirty-something mom who feels like the wrinkles are the most noticeable part of her face! Later that day, I saw my own dad, and he asked me why I would dye my hair black as he gave a look of disapproval (although it wasn't actually black, it was dark brown and very close to the natural color of my hair). It may seem like an insignificant comment to some, but for those who have had years of condemning words from a loved one, even the little comments cut like a knife. A couple of years ago, I would have gone home and cried and wondered why my dad has to continue to hurt me even now, but I know it only hurts me more to let those thoughts linger. Instead of being angry and bitter with him, I chose to focus on the kind comment from my friend's dad instead of the one from my own. I also prayed that God would continue to work in my dad's heart and make him see how much his comments can hurt people.

I like the saying "Holding on to bitterness is like drinking poison and expecting the other person to die." Hate and bitterness can eat you alive. It can cause great emotional turmoil, stress, physical sickness, headaches, anxiety, stomachaches, ulcers, and so on. God would love to heal us if we will let go of the hate and let Him in.

Choosing to forgive is the first step to freedom and a life of joy that we can have in the Lord if we give our hurts to Him.

I pray that through my pain, God gives me more passion for Him. Over time, I am learning to be thankful for my scars. The pain from the wounds of my scars led me to Christ, and for that I will be forever grateful.

Because of my scars, my heart breaks for young girls and women who are hurting from the scars of their past. Our horse-based ministry, Blazin' Saddles, arose because God gave my mom and me a vision—a vision of hurting people coming to a ranch to interact with people and horses who could show them love and help them find the love and freedom in Christ they have been searching for, the freedom we both spent so many years searching for. God made our scars into something beautiful when we let God show us how to use those scars to help other hurting people.

(For more information on our equine therapy ministry, see our website: www.blazinsaddles.org.)

There is a song by I Am They called "Scars." I have loved the song from the first time I heard it, and it brings tears to my eyes every time I hear it.

> Waking up to a new sunrise
> Looking back from the other side
> I can see now with open eyes
> Darkest water and deepest pain
> I wouldn't trade it for anything
> 'Cause my brokenness brought me to You
> And these wounds are a story You'll use
>
> So I'm thankful for the scars
> 'Cause without them I wouldn't know Your heart
> And I know they'll always tell of who You are
> So forever I am thankful for the scars
>
> Now I'm standing in confidence
> With the strength of Your faithfulness

And I'm not who I was before
No, I don't have to fear anymore

So I'm thankful for the scars
'Cause without them I wouldn't know Your heart
And I know they'll always tell of who You are
So forever I am thankful for the scars

I can see, I can see
How You delivered me
In Your hands, In Your feet
I found my victory
I can see, I can see
How You delivered me
In Your hands, In Your feet
I found my victory

I'm thankful for the scars
'Cause without them I wouldn't know Your heart
And I know they'll always tell of who You are
So forever I am thankful for the scars
So forever I am thankful for the scars

I am so thankful that God has shown me His heart through my scars. Although I do not want my scars to define me, I am grateful for what God has shown me through the pain of this life. He has taken my broken, messed-up life and used it for His good. Because of that, I am thankful for my scars.

I Am God's Daughter

My biggest struggle in life and question with my dad is this: "Why have I never been good enough?" I have wasted most of my life trying to measure up to his standards, trying to always say and do the things I think he would want me to, and trying to work hard enough so that I could earn my worth. Instead of trying to live up to God's standards, I've strived to live up to my earthly father's standards.

The good news is, even if I never feel like I am good enough for my dad, I am good enough for God because I have been born again and am covered in the blood of Jesus. I am now the righteousness of God (2 Corinthians 5:21). When we repent and give our lives to Him, little by little, day by day, He molds us into exactly what He created us to be—not perfect, but constantly being molded and shaped into His likeness.

I do believe in his own way, my dad does love me—even if he doesn't always know how to show it the way I wish he could. The last couple of years it seems like he has been trying to mend some of the fences between us. He calls to check up on my family. He helps with construction projects around our farm at no charge. He even has told me he loves me, which I don't think is an easy thing for him to do. He has given me Mother's Day cards and written his own messages saying I'm a good mom and he is thankful for my kids. Even though the hurtful comments still come at times, they are less and less. I believe God is doing a work in him as he attends church and reads his Bible. Although our relationship isn't the daddy-daughter relationship I have always hoped for, I can honestly say that I appreciate and love my dad today. Our relationship will never be perfect because we are both imperfect people, but I am trusting that as God has been doing a work in me, He is also doing a work in him, and I am hopeful that the Lord will finish the work He has started in him: "Being confident of this, that he who began a good work in you will carry it on to completion until the day of Christ Jesus" (Philippians 1:6).

God is using my sweet children to show my dad love as well as teach my dad how to love. I have no doubt he loves my kids, and they sure love their grandpa in return. They yell, "Grandpa!" every time he opens the door. They love going gopher trapping with him, riding the four-wheeler and snowmobile with him, building forts with him, and going on adventures with him. The Lord has been using my innocent children to soften the heart of my dad, helping a lonely, broken man to feel loved, and he is loving them in return!

Loving and feeling loved in return—that is what God wants for us. Even in His infinite holiness, He loves us so much! If we imagine how much we love our children, spouse, parents, siblings, friends, or pets, it is hard to imagine how much more God loves us. It is not comprehendible for me. I cannot fathom anyone loving anyone or anything more than I love my kids. How awesome that I have a Daddy in heaven who loves me much more than I love my children! He cherishes and adores me the way my earthly father can't. I have a Heavenly Father who delights in me (Zephaniah 3:17)!

John 1:12 tells me, "Yet to all who did receive him, to those who believed in his name, he gave the right to become children of God." I am God's child, *His daughter*!

As God's daughter, I can forgive my dad and give my relationship with him to God. Forgiving him doesn't mean accepting his sin or the things he has done as right. It means setting boundaries for myself and my family if I need to. It means letting God handle him so that I can be free to do the things God has called me to do. It means not taking the chains of my past back and letting God show me what He has for my future. It means loving my dad even through the hurt and extending him the grace that my Heavenly Daddy has given me.

Loving Father

As you read through the final chapter of this book, I want you to consider these questions: Where do I go from here? How do I forgive those who have hurt me? Will I start my relationship with Jesus today? How do I let the Lord lead my life?

Your Loving Father is waiting for you today. Whether you are a teenager, a young mother, an empty nester, enjoying your retirement, or in the later stages of life, He wants to take you by the hand and lead you as you move through the rest of this journey called life.

I love the following passage from the book *Thoughts to Make Your Heart Sing* by Sally Lloyd Jones. It paints a beautiful picture in my mind of our Loving Father walking with us each step of the way through our lives, the way He wants to walk with each one of us.

Loving Heavenly Father

God tells us he is the Creator of Heaven and
Earth! The Mighty God!
And says he is a father as well—your Father.
And then he shows us a tender picture
Like a snapshot from his camera.
It's of our God teaching you—his little child
how to walk. Taking you in his arms.
Gently leading you.

All through your life—from beginning to end
God himself teaches you how to walk with him.

He leads you by the hand.

"…I myself taught my people how to walk, leading them along by the hand." Hosea 11:3 (paraphrase based on NLT)

*****

My dear friend, are you ready to let your loving Heavenly Father lead you through your life? He has been waiting patiently for you. Yes, *you*! He loves you so much and would love to start a relationship with you today. Right now! He doesn't expect you to know how. He will teach you as you go. He will help you learn from your mistakes. He will pick you up to hold and comfort you when the trials of life seem like too much to bear. He will bring you more peace and joy than you thought possible. I pray that as you close this book, if you haven't given your life to Jesus, you wouldn't wait another day! I pray you will cry out to your Heavenly Daddy just like I did. Ask Him to forgive the mistakes you have made. Ask Him to heal the hurts and scars in your life. Ask Him to show you what a life in Christ looks like.

Maybe you go to church and go through the Sunday motions. Are you ready to give Him every day of your life? Are you ready to let Him lead you the rest of the week instead of leaving Him at the church after the Sunday service? He wants to be part of your every-day life, every step you take and every decision you make, guiding you as you go. Will you let Him?

Maybe you already have a relationship with Him. Are you ready to take the next step? Are you ready to step out of the boat and do what He is calling you to do? He blesses us beyond belief when we are obedient to what He calls us to do. Are you ready to take that step in obedience today?

I have been praying for you, my friend, praying that as you read the words the Holy Spirit put on my heart to write, you would grow closer to your Heavenly Daddy, you would desire to live your life for Him and for His greater purpose, you would let Him heal your wounds, and one day you can be thankful for your scars, just as I am.

Afterword

Dad,

As I sit to ponder and pray about the words I write to you, I am reminded of the letters I wrote to you from the time I was a little girl and into my adult years. I wonder if you ever read them. I wonder if they tugged on your heartstrings at all. I wonder if you thought about the words I wrote. I may never know if you read them, and I may never know if you read this book, but in case you do, I want you to know that I love you and forgive you for the pain of the past. I am thankful for the things I went through because God has turned them into something beautiful, and I pray that I can help others as I share my story. This is not to condemn you, because I know a lot of my story hurts, but to help others who have similar struggles.

I can see how God is doing a work in you and softening your heart by the way you love Tyla and Jace, and they adore you in return. I can tell you are trying to show me love by helping with projects or chores, going horseback riding with us, and stopping by just to say hi. Please know that your efforts do not go unnoticed.

I want you to know that I pray for you often—I pray that God would heal the hurts you must harbor from your childhood, I pray that you would know how much Jesus loves you and embrace that love so that it overflows from you into the lives of those around you, I pray that you could let go of the bitterness and anger you have held so tightly to for so many years, I pray that alcohol would no longer have any place in your life, and selfishly, I pray that one day I will know without a doubt that you love me and you are proud of the woman I have become in Christ.

The mistakes of the past are in the past, and I am looking forward to what the future holds for both of us. Praying that we seek the Lord and His will for our lives as we live out the rest of our days on earth.

Love,
Your daughter

About the Author

Amanda Tungseth lives in northwest Minnesota on a horse ranch with her husband, Josh, and children, Tyla and Jace. She cares for the horses and other animals on the ranch, gives riding lessons, and trains horses as well as homeschools her children.

She loves Jesus, her family, and the laughter of her children. She enjoys doing chores early in the morning while watching the sunrise, horse camping trips with her family, reading, organizing events, and attending Christian concerts with her family.

She has a passion for horses and a desire to share the Gospel with people. She and her mom, Wendy, started the nonprofit organization Blazin' Saddles, where they use horses to share the love of Jesus with people and minister to those struggling in different areas of life. For more information on their ministry, visit www.blazinsaddles.org.

CPSIA information can be obtained
at www.ICGtesting.com
Printed in the USA
BVHW031512040321
601748BV00001B/1